MW01699763

Book of Stress Releases

Talk To Your Cells

How to Become Your Own Creator

Step-by-Step Instruction Manual

BY

Elaine Croker

Talk To Your Cells
How to Become Your Own Creator

First Edition

Published by Elaine Croker

NATIONAL LIBRARY OF AUSTRALIA CIP DATA

Croker, Elaine (Elaine Grace), 1945- .

Talk to your cells: how to become your own creator.
1st ed.
ISBN 9780646471686 (pbk.).
1. Self-help techniques. 2. Awareness.
I. Title.
158.1

Cover Designed by CleverLink
www.cleverlink.com.au

Printed and bound in Australia by Southwood Press
www.southwoodpress.com.au

Acknowledgements

My thanks goes to my editor and to all those who had so much patience and faith in me as I wrote.

I would also like to thank my clients, students and family who have proven the benefits of the technique and stress releases contained in this book in their everyday lives.

This book is designed as a companion volume to my first book **Talk to Your Cells, and become your own creator**.

It is the instruction manual and provides the "how to" and techniques for changing your life simply by communicating with your cells.

The techniques and stress releases presented in this book have been developed over 14 years of study and practice in my work. The techniques are based on the understanding that our cells are intelligent. If we tell our cells what to do they will help us achieve well being.

My first book **Talk to Your Cells, and become your own creator** contains some of the 100's of success stories of people who have experienced life changing results through these techniques.

This book gives you the tools to transform who you are and enable you to achieve your dreams and aspirations.

Contents

Introduction

This book is a collection of emotional, spiritual and physical stress releases aimed at balancing the three levels of our being; body, mind and soul. The body is our vehicle, our mind is our master and our soul is our destiny.

Our health, wealth and well-being is determined by how well these 3 levels of our being are working together as one.

The three levels of our being respond to what we say and think. This can be positive or negative.

Our subconscious is a willing slave and believes and responds without question to what we say and think. If we say or think we can or cannot do something, either way, the subconscious accepts this as the truth and obeys.

We are all born with the capacity and ability to be healthy, wealthy, and wise. We are the master of our destiny and by programming our cells through the spoken word and our thoughts, we set the vibration of our cells to take us in the direction we have dictated.

Every day brings new opportunities. As new cells are created and old cells are discarded we can renew and reaffirm our ambitions and dreams.

When we speak our vision, energy patterns arise that will obey our commands and produce what we have declared.

Our cells are wise. They hold the wisdom of our life force. We can communicate with our cells to determine what we or our body needs to achieve good health and well being.

Every day our sub-conscious mind (our cells) are waiting, for direction from us. Our subconscious mind is listening to our words and thoughts in order to understand and materialise what is our true reality in life.

Let go, and have faith in the power that is within you. May you become the master of your cells and creator of you.

The World's Energies

There are eight energies that exist around and through us and make our existence on the earth possible. They are:

Magnetic Energy

This is an energy that is balanced from the North and South Poles and telepathically carries vibrations across the earth.

It is magnetic energy that allows our cells to maintain contact with each. Every cell has a north and south pole. One cell's south poll is attracted to and is joined to the next cell's north pole.

Sound vibration is carried via magnetic energy enabling the cells to receive and respond to sound energy.

Our cells are talking all the time. Every cell knows all there is to know, it is a universal programme that never changes and all life forms understand its data.

CELL VIBRATIONS

We are born to hear, think and act. Whatever we hear can change us if we believe in it. Even sickness is sometimes simply a suggestion from somewhere.

Our cells grow in accordance with suggestions and what we believe in and can create healthy or unhealthy bodies and emotions.

Since this body of ours hears all that we say and obeys all our instructions, it is wise to speak only what is healthy and good for us and our body of cells.

We must be careful in our beliefs and our words. Everything in our world is involved in this dialogue with our cells. When we know we deserve the best and we speak it, we will find that our cells will do all in their power to make our dreams come true.

This is true for the three things we all deserve – health, wealth and happiness.

Atomic Calendar

Atomic energy is generated by the moon's cycles throughout our lunar monthly calendars.

We are born under a calendar that follows the moon's cycles. The power of the moon affects so many things apart from the ocean's tides. If we understand it, we can use it wisely.

Our emotions change with our hormonal balance and this balance changes in accord with each lunar month. Every cell is affected by the pull of the moon.

If you start something when the moon is waxing, it will be more successful than if you begin after the full moon, when the lunar power is waning.

LIGHT ENERGY

Light energy is radiation and ultra violet patterns generated by the Sun. The sun passes over us every day and every cell within us uses the light to develop and live with health and energy.

Nothing grows without sunshine, including us. When the sky is overcast or if it is raining, our liver is the organ that substitutes the effect of sunlight through our liver enzymes.

It is our backup. We can replace our light force by realizing this, and programming our cells to be filled with sunlight every day.

KINETIC ENERGY

The opposing and transforming energies of Yin and Yang balance and feed our meridians. Its basis is the balance between us and the trees. The trees are the Yin and we are the Yang.

Positive and Negative Ionisation

We breathe oxygen into every cell. If we did not, the cell would die and so would we. Our recycling breath forms the power to replenish our world.

Let's know the power to breathe as we should and every cell will respond. Health and Well Being is ours by the way we breathe the breath of life.

Gravity

The gravitational energy of the earth pulls everything back to her ensuring that all our toxic waste is recycled through her system.

We stand on the outside of the earth. We walk on her surface and never fall off.

This magic energy allows nothing to go astray. Every part of us goes back to the ground. Our waste and toxins pass through us towards the ground.

If we are balanced right, every waste product will be gravitated to pass through us.

Today most of us wear shoes that block the positive effects this energy should have on our health and wellbeing.

It is wise to stand on the ground and allow ourselves to be re-grounded and therefore cleansed of our toxins and waste.

Positive Energy via Water

Water was the life force of all planetary forms until we learned how to breathe oxygen from air.

Moving water, from rivers, oceans and lakes, creates electricity and this electricity is our life force, our kundalini. It lights up our cells. Our mind uses this energy to think and form actions.

These energies are ours to call upon and use as we wish. This stress release book is primed into using them for you. Just choose your numbers and read the stress release out loud, knowing life gave you the right to make all your dreams come true.

Our values and belief systems are designed to create our future. Things change as we humans develop. We all can achieve our goals and make our dreams come true. The breath of life is in us all. We can tap into our reserves and the knowledge and skills held in potential in our cells and achieve greatness.

I have over the last fifteen years formed the power of Prime Tuning our human cells by understanding the cellular vibrations. This allows all of our cells to work in harmony to produce the best possible results.

There is nothing to stop us having all that we dream and desire once we have talked from our higher self to our trillions and trillions of cells.

These cells come from a seed that developed through our gestation. We come from a genetic pool of life, waiting to be conceived as a human.

We are made from a collection of genetic patterns that have all the past in them. This is formed into a mind that can think, talk and act with its own memories coded from that genetic pool. This knowledge opens the power of the present moment and allows us to use all our potential.

Every cell is a care taker of our feelings, our ideals, and our future. These tiny cells wait for us to tell them what we plan to do, then they act as telepathic transmitters, communicating across all borders and bringing in all the energies we need to achieve our aims.

Money is energy forming over and over again. We spend money to give money to someone else. That will allow them to spend it allowing it to travel back to us.

Diseases and sickness are simply cells that have lost their power to be healthy. Negative emotions and stress build doubts and fears. This allows cells to wear your stress, thus giving you stressful cells.

When we use a stress release, these cells move on through the system and allow the new cells space to repair and become well again.

All you need to do is to allow all these tiny cells to grant it to you.

How to Talk to your Cells

When you talk to your cells, you are talking to your sub-conscious mind. Your cells and sub-conscious mind are one.

The principle of talking to your cells to change your life is to instruct your cells to behave as you choose.

The subconscious mind does not understand humour, inference or sub-text so it is important your communication with your subconscious mind is always clear and concise.

The idea is to send these instructions through your frontal brain that allows the energy to enter through the blood flowing into the brain.

Let yourself leave it to the left and right brain to process your intent. Don't get involved.

To become the master of your cells perform the following simple steps:

1. Think of the subject you wish to balance or improve such as; find a new job, change your health or reduce stress

2. Think of a number between 1 and 95 and note down the first number that comes to mind. If more than one number comes into your mind, note them down in the order you thought of them

3. Locate the stress release in the following section of this book that corresponds with the number you thought of. For example if you thought of 21, you would open the book to Stress Release 21

4. Hold your thumbs on both sides of your temples, and then place your four fingers down the midline of your forehead as illustrated in Figure 1. This technique stimulates the glands of your brain so that they can receive and respond to the instructions in the stress release

5. Read the Stress Release you have selected to yourself slowly and clearly
6. Take a deep breath and breath out after reading each stress release

Note; if you thought of and noted down more then 1 number, repeat steps 3 – 5 for each number in the order you thought of them.

FIGURE 1: STRESS RELEASE TECHNIQUE

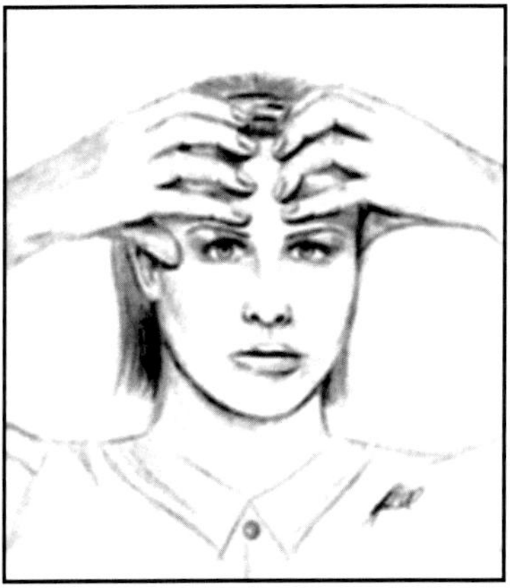

Just before bedtime is a good time to do stress release and programming, for as you sleep the body will change the cells around ready for the next day.

If you are sitting an exam, applying for a new job, or buying something for yourself, this will blend with your stress release and work through you to bring the results.

Energy will flow your way and so will the people who will help you in your quest.

Every time you do a stress release, your body must make changes to fulfil your plans. This means that your body will need to work itself into what you've asked of it.

It is therefore important to eat as your instinct tells you, because your five senses are involved in this change.

You will begin to know how you should act and what you should do, where you should go to get everything you need. You must rely on your intuition and instinct for this. It is communication with your subconscious in every cell of your body.

Don't let your old habits and belief systems run your new life. You can re-programme yourself time and time again, but remember, every time you do so you must wait for your body to adjust.

Always be sure that you know what you're aiming for, and I promise you from my own experience and that of my clients, that what you ask for, you will get.

95 Life Changing Stress Releases

"I am"
the master of all my cells.

I now ask every cell to balance itself so that my plans achieve reality. As I let the energy flow through me, I allow my mind to concentrate on my acts so they relate with my self esteem to work and form me, as the captain in charge.

I love and honour myself and know that everything I plan will be completed by me. I ask for my emotions to change to suit this concept.

I shall give to receive, and I have no doubts, nor will I believe in failure. I have the receipt for the success of my plan because I have already received what I have decided to claim.

It has become my reality.

"I am"
the master of my cells.

I now ask for my cells to work through the space of my labour to create the body pattern I need for this creative work.

Increase the flow of energy in every cell making the whole of me supportive and give me the results I desire.

I ask for my blood to use its liver amino acids to my advantage. Let each endorphin work through the liver to create the hormones needed for this task.

Let my mind focus with the glands correctly, so the increased energy is controlled precisely.

I love and honour myself knowing I will use this power holistically to create what I've asked of myself. I will select the right emotions so that the programme is proven.

I will complete this task.

"I am"
the master of my cells.

I love and honour this fact. I ask every cell to balance me into my dream. I ask for everything that will draw the outside vision to come into the centre of my "I Am".

Allow the focus of my intention to create happiness for myself and everyone around me. Let my higher self not trade with past mistakes or beliefs, but bring the old into a new common sense. I love the results this brings to all of us.

I shall increase the flow of emotional energy needed to achieve my aims. As I build this dream, I know I am free and so is everyone else involved.

I will not trade in other people's opinions to gain information, but will nurture my own inspiration and accept all the loving support offered to me.

I will successfully achieve my goals.

"I am"
the master of my cells.

I now ask every cell to focus on my goal. My endorphins will increase and my energy levels will change accordingly. Every muscle within me will work in step with my consciousness.

As I hear the sounds of thought, I ask for the cells to empower that thought via the engineering of my glands and fuels. I will use what my body has in stock to build my cells with sound therapy.

I ask for the liver to reinforce the glucose that energises the flow of hormones throughout the performance I am embarking on.

Let every nerve relate correctly to the higher consciousness. The result will bounce through the telepathic signals of the brain and into the cells successfully.

"I am" the master of my cells. I shall achieve my desired result.

"I am"
the master of my cells.

I now focus on my glands that shall increase my engineering to create a masterminded cell that will empower my dreams.

Every muscle is a pump for my blood and as the flow passes through them, let the lactic acids be transported correctly.

Let my heart pump with the kidneys so that fluids move on without draining the organs of life. I easily adapt to many changes occurring at the one time, and will not allow my past to colour my future.

Let all my cells understand that my mind is already victorious. I have already received what my imagination has created. My emotions know the power of achievement.

I will complete this accomplishment.

"I am"
the master of my cells.

I now ask for every cell to bring me into a sense of well being with all of its friends. Let every cell know its right to enjoy the telepathic voices of peaceful humanity.

Let every other cell involved know that the cells belonging to me are balanced. I will not judge the cells of other people but know who "I am".

Let every challenge not be a drama, but a conquest into a peaceful result. Let all the emotions involved trade honestly with each other.

Therefore I shall be blessed and so shall they, untied by the bonding of;

Love, Joy, Grace, Peace and Wisdom.

"I am"
the master of my cells.

I love and honour them all. As I focus the importance of my goal to find myself completely happy, I ask the sane side of their memories to balance me.

Allow the forces of my thinking to bond with my higher self that will achieve this balance. Let each gene within these cells focus with me, so that I can use them to overcome all challenges.

Let them not be cursed or judged by me against the past, but touch the inmost reaches of my mind and relate it with "The Now".

Let them love me, and so I shall love them. Each old emotion will be remodelled into "The Now" , achieving the happiness we can all share.

"I am"
the master of these cells.

I bring them into communication with the inner child and my dreams. The inner child in me will grow and mature with me. I am the creator of all its energies.

I am aware of past generations still living in me, but I will not allow them to curse this lifetime and my inner child.

I will protect and love my inner child always. This gives me the power to move on and not look backwards.

Let the negative emotions of my ancestral genes that cling to me be changed without harming the gene's integrity. The past is not offended, but remodelled into the now.

I and my inner child love them and their life force because they are my very own flesh and blood.

"I am"
the master of my cells.

I now allow my consciousness to believe in my chosen lifestyle. As the stress of my timetable becomes greater, let me not over react but work through it calmly.

Let every emotion involved not force fatigue nor allow any loss of self-esteem. Let the cells understand my every need and stand by me so that I am prepared beforehand for every situation.

It will therefore be successful. I know and understand the way my body normally works, so let every cell now work more fully with me to feed the energy needed for my career.

I have the memory bank of my forefather's dreams, so let them see me do what I've planned. Open my brain to understand that it's not by remembering, but by knowing, so the outcome is already successful.

"I am"
the master of my cells.

I love and care for my innermost powers and can relax with my emotions. My body of cells form the correct amount of natural enzymes to carry the elements through the wall of every cell.

I breathe in and out continuously, letting the cells release the spent carbon dioxide, taking the burnt-out emotions with it.

As I breathe, let me feel completely practical. I have then let go of whatever was improper for my own sense of reality.

I am free to be myself in whatever I do, or say.

"I am" now happy.

"I am"
the master of my cells

but I have been allowing them to form incorrectly and create problems for me. I now allow these problems to be addressed, therefore drying up the emotions that created them and caused me pain and sorrow.

Now that I understand why I made a contract with the offending emotions, I can happily ask them to leave.

Let me not judge myself or others. I now understand that my cells were not grounded until I faced my own situation and saw the relationship I had with the offender

We are now freed by this stress release.

"I am"
the master of my emotions.

As I balance my relationship with my emotions, I become attuned to the "I am". I know that I will find the power of common sense working through me.

Everyone I meet with will see me as having a stable personality. I have no incorrect feelings that would judge my fellowman.

I live and am rewarded by every cell.

I am fulfilled and happy.

"I am"
the master of my cells.

I have every right to live out the ideals that come to me. Let this power open a creative sense of well being in me and I shall grow as a true child of life by everyone's reality.

Let me know my joys to their fullest. May my love cherish every moment I live.

“I am” now united with this power that rebirths itself in and through me to gather together people of the same ideals. I shall rejoice and my name will be blessed. "I am" all things to me.

I have every right to be me.

"I am"

the colleague who learns from the fountain of life.

I love and honour the role I have embarked upon. My human senses are now engaged with the universal forces that will channel through me to teach me my lifestyle.

The values I now hold are planned into my thought patterns. As I think, I believe it shall happen. As I stand still to programme this concept into my human cells, I let my mind hold my plan completed with me standing adorned with its gifts already received.

I shall enjoy every step that I now take to make it come true through me.

"I am"

the interested buyer and seller of my concept.

I adore its right to be mine. I found it as I searched for the right thing to own. Now let my resources match the same levels as my vision.

I honour my own senses that will grant me the grounding to insist on my ownership of this concept.

Let all emotions involved be valued and blended so that everyone is completely happy with the results.

I am not procrastinating about the problems, but engineering my cells to relate with the trader, the seller and the receiver.

All are blessed by the outcome.

"I am"
the reality of a new career.

The secrets of my breast are laid bare. I can now work with an inner desire that's part of my natural skills, given to me from my higher self.

I ask for my genes to recognise this right, and to form a balance on my behalf. I love this power to increase my telepathic signals that would connect with someone looking for me at that level of thinking.

Allow all my body to then portray the features of my skills through my posture, smile, speech and dress sense.

I shall then find what I desire. I shall be discovered by the people who will help me build my new career.

"I am"
my own caretaker.

I will walk into a new reality of my higher self. I shall balance every cell to accept this concept with safety. I will use my powers to care for this body through all dangers involved with this journey.

No one can shake my faith in my ability and skills to do so. I have both time and money to create the capsule of trust that marks my cells to enter the contest. Let me love every stage of its trials that will bring me out the other side victorious.

My ideals will yield fourfold!

"I am"

the soul who has the right to have a memory book signed by me.

Let my life form this wonderful reality that will write on the pages. There will be no mistakes amongst these cherished memories. I love being born into a genetic lineage that selected my gifts and talents through trial and error.

I am the consciousness that will now take the tools and write. Let all my emotions and gifts be balanced to write a perfect story.

I have already received an invoice and I shall pay the bill in full. I am now ready to accept my purchase of this blank book.

The story I am writing is for myself and what I plan to be.

"I am"

the power of the divine nature.

I have the soul of this powerful journey in me. I see what I am in a valued trust fund willed to me and signed as mine when I come of age.

The door to the outside world opens to a balanced field where many games are played.

Let me go forth through that door and seek my future. I will then come home honoured by having played my cards right, with the divine nature I grew up with under the family name.

Let my honoured return be a joy to all my folk and family, as I present myself matured and trustworthy.

"I am"
the single eye of my consciousness.

I am responsible for the way I do things. Let me now balance myself so my ideals come true.

I am not governed by luck, fate or pride. I am the result of the learning patterns that came through me from my elder's wisdom. I am not of their time, but in my time I shall use this earth to form good from evil.

I will light up the darkness with the torch in my hand that was given to me in their trust. I shall show them the way into a new earth pattern of light, magnified for their resurrected consciousness being lived once again in me as their common reality.

"I am"

the master of the energy fields known as the Christ helix that designed the cell seeds that created each human mind.

This allows me to use the incoming power to reinforce my healing consciousness. Let the cells of my being light up the power that will heal the world of sickness and infirmities.

These Christ powers are the consciousness of faith that knows the spoken word can Create miracles.

I was formed to have the power to use this ability to heal. As the cells of life form in me, I know that cures will come through faith, in tune with life and fed and watered by the power of the spoken word.

"I am"

the balanced consciousness that will direct the flow of life into a powerful form of healing.

I will light up the life force and burn out all sick cells. A new cell will fill the place that has been cleansed by the energy of potash.

Let the life force balance the new cells so they are nurtured by healthy fodder and fluids. Open the electromagnetic fields and energise them with the correct ratio of cell to cell vibrations.

Make every cell unique and let it vibrate with health, grounded and stabilised through Mother Earth.

"I am"

the caretaker of the inner powers that will open the holistic right to be engineered as a healthy human being.

I ask for all cells to be fed the elements that shall give each cell the main proteins and energy to fuel a luminous life.

Let this then light up the auric flare around every cell that will blend with it to heal the light body. Let me live in this light body until my physical body returns itself to good health.

I will then be completely cured.

"I am"
my sickness.

My emotional trials made me so. I am now conscious of the emotional powers inside my life force that made me create the imbalance that made me sick.

Let my body now realise this and open the cells that are sick and dismiss such emotional turmoil. I shall then leave behind the chaos of those emotions.

Let me now create good health inside me. I invited the emotions that dropped in to harm me, so now I ask them to leave, none offended by my saving grace I have saved myself from their dangerous games.

"I am"

the power of building a new cell, correcting the sickness of my organs.

I will deal with a dumb cell inside me. This is a cell that's mounted onto another cell taking its life forces to live on.

I have made this cell from a chemical mistake that changed the vibration of the healthy cell into an incorrect pulsing.

This has resulted in the misuse of the elements and chemistry of my cells, therefore affecting the organs.

I now re-programme these organs so they replace only those cells that are not cloned from the dumb cells, therefore I shall replace myself, cured.

"I am"
the master of my cells.

My consciousness formed a cell that is stricken with Candida. This is a form of emotional sweating around the cells involved.

I ask for my inner powers to now cleanse the emotions and form a body wash that will wash each cell clean of Candida.

I will now eat and drink as my body tells me therefore purifying the water inside my body.

I will work with the whole of my body and it will be given the cure. I will now clean up Candida from my physical form. I also clean my aura and my soul of this inferiority complex.

"I am"

the bower bird that collected emotions that created my troubles.

I ask to understand why I did this to myself. I will not play games or judge why it's so. I will clear the emotions by myself.

I now take them off my cells and thereby relieve my boiling painful feelings. Let my body breathe in to relate with my incoming consciousness, then I will breathe out all the wrong emotions that I have collected over the years.

I am now free to live my personal life corrected.

"I am"
the pure senses of my truths.

I am not obliged to another's truth. I produce the energy formulas that create my behaviour.

No other person's concept can mark my brow with guilt. I do know that my behaviour must relate to a personal standard.

Let me consider the bigger picture, and as I work with my truths, I will respect other people's truths and never judge from my point of truths.

This will set me free to work with everyone without contempt, judgement or favour. I shall enjoy this human harmony.

"I am"
the master of my cells.

I have this powerful ability to arrange my own mental thinking. I allow myself to ask from myself what I must complete as I focus with who I desire to become. Let this human body build the cells within me to create the energy and performance I've decided to use.

Bring up the knowledge within me that is stored from my forefathers' experiences. Then let me bless their way into myself, for they are to be part of me.

"I am" the power that is then blended with their souls to increase the finished master pages of life that's continuous.

"I am"
my soul mate on my pilgrimage.

I love and honour the values inside its transit. If I can know this path of life through the common sense of my being, allow me now to make peace with its life force. Let me change the flow of events that would hinder my truths.

"I am" holding now every one of my forefathers' genes as a trustee. I have this earth timetable with everything that's been before me, so now let me go forth to discover what will enhance it and perfect it.

I have enough love, light and common sense to release their genes from all old scarring.

"I am"
the master of these cells.

Through my human senses I know what this earth means to me. I understand everything that ever was, and that gives me the ability to be part of her soul. I will help her promises become true.

Let me be wise and strong when I write my name and lifetime into the "Book of Life".

She is "The Footstool" of my creator's dreams, the source of all learning. I am the consciousness of all my cells and through them I will reach out and walk by faith in this earth's new regime.

I have the freedom to translate creation's promises and make them come true.

"I am"

the results of the seeds of my forefathers.

All my memories are connected to them. I now ask for a new translation of the master's plan.

My consciousness will resurrect them into a new heaven on earth. Let me stand before the altar of life and take their hand to lead them to freedom.

I will hear their voices reveal their visions and they will trust me to set them free. I understand that this is the greatest stage for the earth's pilgrimage.

I now have their approval to release them because they are of me and I am of them.

We are one in the Creator's image.

"I am"

the star of the play of my destiny

I am also the writer and director. Let me portray the magic of my life using goodness and not evil. Let every cell support my performance and mature my Inner Child. I shall perform my role with grace, using light, love and healing to bind all scenes together.

Let all that I say be imbued with the energy of acceptance and love, creating a vision of fellowship without judgement.

I am now involved in this life, using Christlike healing. I am refilling the world with God's vision.

"I am"
the right person for myself.

I trust myself to do what is right for me. As I set each personal goal, I ask all my cells to support me in that goal. They shall be blessed by me.

Let everyone who would share a portion of me in some way, learn from me the goodness of sharing with complete trust. We are all then committed to success.

I am but one part of the future. The whole is made up of everyone. All our skills and energy must unite.

We will then share the results holistically.

"I am"
the master of my cells.

I have the power to make my dreams come true. I love and honour the privilege to ask for myself everything that will model my dreams into reality.

Let my emotions be appropriate for my opportunities. As I think of my plan, let me carefully place every detail in its proper position.

I own this plan, I am its master, I value it and will create it successfully.

"I am"
the master of my cells.

My energy will allow me to uphold my human ideals.

Let my whole body of cells cling to this human as a growing vine would spread itself across the wall for support. I am the trellis that will hold the vine where my fruit will ripen to be picked in season.

I know that I will yield fruit that the master of my harvest asked of me. It will be perfect; a true, certified result from pure seed.

"I am"
the consciousness of my future.

I will make the right decisions. I will have the right energy. I will use goodness to achieve the best results.

My mind is the power that will create the fulfilment of my dreams. I shall breathe life into it. I will use light and wisdom to train my future. My emotions must support it in a positive way.

I shall enjoy every part I play in my future growth and the attainment of my dreams.

"I am"
the pattern of the future.

I love and cherish myself and will be whoever I want to be. It is the way I think that will work out the angles that will create my successful portfolio.

I will not let my emotions get in the way. I can therefore do it with ease. As I learn more skills I become more energised and wise.

I have no worries or stress about my progress. I will hold the right position as a result of my faith in my abilities.

"I am"
the master of my cells.

I create my own wishes. I wish for myself. Let me now build the energy around me so that I can believe in myself.

I have the abundance to purchase this wish. I shall meet the right people and gather around me all the encouragement to strive for that wish.

I shall work to make the wish come true

"I am"
the master of my cells.

I am a professional being. I shall receive guidance to develop. I ask my body to look and feel professional. I ask every emotion to give me daily balance in my work.

I am already successful. I ask the trading spirits around me to stay out of my professional actions and performance.

I shall train those that work by my side with a good rapport.

Our results will be well paid for, both for them and for me.

"I am"
the result of my stories.

I must understand the power of the energy in everything I say. My words will create my future so let me now declare clearly all that I desire.

I shall bring every detail into focus, using the truths that tell my story correctly.

Therefore all those around me will receive a gift from my vision. What I say, so shall I receive.

We shall all reap the providence Of My Words.

"I am"
the master of my cells.

I am my best friend in the study of my path through life. I will gather friends along the way who will teach me to value "who I am".

As I come into a new consciousness as a human being, let me learn "who I am" for the benefit of everyone.

I shall create new friendships as a lifetime gift, the gift that brought me my truths.

Let the pages turn over every day, teaching me what I should know about myself, without harming or distorting another's rights to be themselves.

I shall then love who they are without judgements or distortion of my own truths.

"I am"
a colleague in the new learning field.

I re-establish myself successfully through all my changes of direction by being integrated with my human. All these changes will happen without stress of worry.

My vibrations will lift with my new vision and direction. I shall meet the people I need to learn from and enjoy the feelings this will bring.

I now balance myself to be level with their way of thinking. My values will be as high as theirs. I will become as mature as they are.

The skills of my chosen field will come easily and quickly to me as I learn to mix with this good community of people.

"I am"
the master of my cells.

I can manifest my dreams to change the direction in my career. I will discover all I need to know for this change. The information I need I will read and understand without fear of failure.

My feelings will blend with my desires and I will receive the changes in my career gladly.

I am balanced into my new career without any fear.

"I am"
strong in my new career.

I am safe to do what is expected of me. I will fulfil my vision to be wanted and useful for everyone who works with me.

May this be through the power of trust. I shall learn quickly the things I should know, and then everything I do will come to me freely and I will do it well.

The door to this success is open to me. I have created this opportunity and I shall be rewarded with an abundant lifestyle.

This new career and lifestyle is mine and I am already successful.

"I am"
right for my career.

My truth will balance with my results and will support my new lifestyle. The people I mix with will find me right and trustworthy in my dealings with them.

Let all my days blend with my new future, without stress or incorrect changes. Let my body posture and facial expression show me upright and interested in my career.

My words will flow naturally and will open my self-seeded dream box and allow it to flourish with my care.

I am now valued and valuable to the people I work with.

"I am"
the master of my cells.

I trust in my ability to choose properly the new staff I need. Let the people who join my workforce come with good feelings about the space they will occupy in my company.

I have the power to relate firmly and fairly and my staff will be happy to work for me for our joint success.

This shall come by my being balanced with life and my own destiny, fulfilling the dreams I have created.

All my staff will have a lifestyle of a high standard, furnished with honesty and enjoyment.

We will all live the success together.

"I am"
a new staff member in this firm.

I ask to balance my feelings and values for success. Let me be honest in my dealings with my staff and workmates.

I can be relied on and will fulfil the expectations of those above me. I will create expectation at the highest level.

I am the right person for everyone who will rely on me to safely bring their dreams for this company to fruition.

I love my work and the creation of my new reality.

"I am"
the master of my cells.

I believe I can do whatever I decide to do. I now release any emotional influences that would drain me of achieving my goal.

Let me not be confused by asking for incorrect emotions to influence me. Let me be true only to myself.

I have made a contract with my belief, and therefore it is mine because I believe so.

"I am"
greater than my fears.

I now declare that I am ready to accept myself as I am. Let any emotions that would play games with me now leave.

Today I stress release all negative emotions and fear. I am now restored and I will create a new stress free me.

I will then have the power to be whatever I declare myself to be.

I now have the goodwill to achieve greater and greater things for myself united correctly through me because;

I have cured myself of fear.

"I am"
filled with a new vision.

I see myself assembling the foundations of a future full of options. Let me learn quickly what choices I have and which is the right choice for me.

I will focus on the correct door, and I will walk through it and learn all that I need to become more than before.

Let every cell inside me then become this vision and use the skills of my forefathers, gifted to me by their genetic memory, free from any negative emotions.

My lifetime dream is coming true.

"I am"
ready to accept my new career.

I am balanced and ready for it. My inner self is strong and healthy and allows me to complete all my daily tasks.

I have the energy to do many things each day, without fatigue or stress. My emotions will keep me happy in my work and keep my workmates happy with me.

We will all be relaxed and efficient while undertaking each task.

I will support them, and they will support me in all our work.

We will all be successful.

"I am"
totally responsible for my career.

Therefore every cell in me must balance as one in support of this. Every part of my body then works as I plan to create every act is successful and in accord with my desires.

Each day brings me to higher levels in my career, and each day I grow emotionally and technically in support of that growth.

I have already chosen to be successful as my career grows.

I am the master of my own success.

"I am"

the human who supports my soul that planned to work in this field. I apply all of me to nurture my soul.

I will work through every step necessary for success in this field and all involved in my work will support me.

Let my thoughts bond with the soul matrix, and include all of the earth's people in the rewards my work will bring.

Let us not pollute the economy or the earth, but share in her wealth.

I am good for this contract because I am

Healthy, Wealthy, and Wise.

"I am"

a consciousness who does not fear the changes the earth plans to take us through.

I will lift up my thinking and create her values through my mind. I am in tune with the earth and I balance intuition and common sense on her behalf.

I will not allow the chanting of negative spirits talk through me. I am growing beyond past traumatic belief systems and I will strengthen my lifestyle and creations to suit her new vision.

We are the motifs for the future.

"I am"
the master of my cells.

The soul created my consciousness for its growth. I take total responsibility for who I am.

Let me now rise above the death angels that previously controlled and processed my soul and forced it to repay karmic debts.

Let me, in this lifetime break the cycle that would otherwise recreate pain and loss in future incarnations.

I can now love myself enough to focus my dreams to build my empire in this lifetime. I shall leave the past behind me now and tread my own pathway, freed from spiritual dramas and their influences.

I am now free. I will live in this modern world, happy and fulfilled.

"I am"
myself in the form of a human being.

I understand that this form is the image and result of the Creator's dreams.

I therefore have the power to read his mind and work towards his ideals on this earth. In this way I live a true and upright existence.

I enjoy the concept and actuality of the Creator and me, enfolded together as one.

The human and the mind that made the human therefore work as one.

Together we create the ideals and build this earth as one, Body, Mind and Soul.

"I am"
the master of my cells.

My focus is the greatest force in my world. It is I who translate my own power to be used for or against me.

My life is the essence of my future in heaven and earth. Allow me to give of my best as the earth spins throughout time.

Let our soul know that we are the saving grace that can change this time into what it will become.

Then allow every cell within us to create and balance the energy for good.

Our combined focus will bring the promised millennium into fruition.

"I am"
the master of my cells.

A new fountain of life is surging through me. I have the formulas that will condense its energy and translate it into practical reality.

Let each cell within me charge up its aura so that I will attract everything that will make human energy fields work via the matrix.

Let me know the consciousness of this formula. It is part of a new era where the earth will trade to uphold peace and perfection for all mankind.

"I am"
myself.

I own the consciousness that understand the power that can lift mankind into the realm of the essence of everything.

Therefore I can telepathically translate all incoming messages that will open the doors for mankind to relate to the Soul.

We are then the master of our flesh, reflecting our light body to create a rainbow for the soul.

Let every cell within me know it is happening so I can then personally open my Book of Life.

I will read all its knowledge and turn it into wisdom for me.

"I am"

the full spectrum of all colours of the earth cells.

Their rainbow is my fountain of life. My aura explains me as the aura of all beings and cells explain them.

I therefore have the right to communicate telepathically with all life forms on this earth.

Open my inner ear to tune with all vibrations from all species. I will then understand all stages of the soul's growth.

I have the power to understand and bring all soul forms, from all life forces, into the magic of communication and evolution.

"I am"
the master of my cells.

I must value my time on this earth. I can add to my life's experiences by discovering what the earth has for me.

Let each cell that came with me now own this moment. Let me be still in it, and understand my power to create the whole of existence in this one still moment of time.

I now know and understand why I am here in this human form.

My task is to reveal the mind of the Creator, through understanding my own mind.

"I am"
the vessel that was made from clay.

I have a spirit in me. I have a soul and an angel of light. Since I am made of clay, to reclothe the spirit, the soul, the angel and I can become whatever I plan to be.

These cells of clay will instruct the soul and clothe it in the correct emotions.

I shall change without stress. By faith, I will climb to the summit of the highest mountain and cross the valleys with ease.

I shall sail the oceans without mishap and arrive at my destiny.

I will reconnect with my entire lineage and take the best into my future.

"I am"
the master of my cells.

I can create a new expectation of my dreams. I must use the power of my mind to tune every cell within me into my whole.

The vision I create for my future will use the emotions that will fulfil the dream.

I shall do it in this lifetime. I shall love my Inner Child enough to let it grow up and become a matured human being within all of my cells.

I am then whole and completed. I shall achieve what I set out to do.

"I am"
the result of my belief systems.

I behave in accordance with these standards. I have inside me my Book of Life.

In this book my story is already written. Let me open it without reference to my standards then I shall find the real "I am".

I will open the pages and read my directions. I will make every word declare my true values.

I can then open my heart and feel good about myself and know that I will live out this life successfully.

"I am"
the Genesis of my future.

Let my soul, my angel of light, my spirit and my human mind bond with my flesh to create me worthy.

Let me work through myself to add everything that will cause all who love me to do so without emotional dramas.

I shall relate with earth, heaven and every planetary form. They are all part of me.

Let every cell I use go back to the earth well spent.

Then every memory will be sanctified by me.

STRESS RELEASE 67

"I am"
the colour chart of my own aura.

I have every shade of all colours. I love and form these colours through my emotions. Their power means my actions are always timely.

When I act to turn my dreams into physical creation, my aura will reflect each colour, thereby enhancing the energy and force of my commitment to making my dreams a reality.

My values are cloaked with life and intention, shown through the colours of my aura being; blue, green, aqua, lemon, gold, orange, red, rose pink, violet purple, silver, and turquoise all blended to create "Pearl white".

"I am"
the visual pattern of my aura.

I have every shade of all colours. These are my shield and protection.

This aura is a body of light that touches and protects the outside edge of my being.

Let me be aware of this energy everywhere I go so I will not walk into danger.

Therefore I am safe from all things that would harm my physical self. I communicate with this protective shield I have produced to surround me.

Let my mind direct my actions in accordance with the prompts from my aura.

I shall then not be hurt or harmed in any way.

"I am"
the coloured chart of my dreams.

Through this I am connected with everyone I love. Let the colours flow and bond with the heart chakra. Bring green and silver through the metallic consciousness of all chakra colours.

I now invite my loved ones to dine with me in my haven of colours. We shall laugh together, love and deal honestly with each other.

I will say the right things and they will hear what they need to hear. In this way they will know what is right for them to share with me.

This aura is my everlasting home. It is of me and made by me for them to enjoy being with me.

"I am"

the coloured mirror that will reflect the light of the sun and create a powerful energy conduit.

This coloured cone of light will recharge my cells with energy.

Let me now work through each cell to ensure that all cells include light forms in this body of fluids.

Let each element that made the cells be charged with light in tandem with its coded formulas. Let this be fuel that will burn up and spark the life-force I need for my actions.

Thus I am the flow of Light, Life, and Actions.

My dreams will now come true.

"I am"
all my colours.

They will blend and encourage my desired actions. This rainbow is a powerful creative tool when I use it with force and direction. Let these colours bond with me at this time to create powerful actions.

Let me stand inside the spike of this coloured bow, and as I feel all my cells fill up with its energy, I shall then achieve whatever I desire.

It is already made, created by the colour energy coursing through me.

Let every cell now contain this coloured light, and then nothing can harm or destroy me or my creation.

"I am"
the coloured cells

that were elected to give me my Forefathers' genes. Let me use these cells in the right way for this changed time on the earth.

I have been entrusted to lift these genes out of death and failures. I will create my own vision without the fear, phobias or old formulas and beliefs that held them hostage.

Let me blend this coloured light force with increased mind power. This will teach me a new way to pass on my forefather's genes, free of outdated ways.

Let then the dead souls be washed from their past in light and colour through me.

"I am"

the coloured form of a new sense of life in earth's new timetable.

I am known by every spirit, soul and guide. It is important for me to uphold the human conscience, which is common sense from the reasoning brain.

Let all incoming messages from every dimension come to me, but then let me change and cloak them in coloured light, reflected from me.

Let my light body touch all the life forms and turn them into human format. Then, as the image of the Creator, we shall wash everything in coloured light and it will blend with the light body we were promised would clothe us.

"I am"
the master of my cells.

My aura flares with every thought knowing everything I think about will change the colours in my aura.

This light will connect to the spiritual senses of my emotions and act through and from me, creating my life's actions.

Let me now know the changes I need to make in my thinking. I will then have clarity in my aura as I use my thoughts for positive outcomes.

I am as I think, created by colours and light.

"I am"
the master of my cells.

I live in a coloured frame that surrounds the pattern of my career. Every day I shall work with the colours that will bring me creative success.

I ask for my aura to protect me from all negative spirits. Let those that I work with have the same colour formulas as me so that our work will flourish.

These colours will form the magic performances I desire and it is my right to bring together everyone involved.

Together we will find that all is achieved correctly.

"I am"
the coloured fax machine

that receives the magic band of colours and wraps them around my dreams.

Let me accept the magic of my forefathers' souls that will help and nurture my body of cells as it prepares the fulfilment of my dreams.

Let all incoming emotional messages to me now be checked and censored so there are no repeats of karmic paybacks.

I then have the true powers of the Christ that told us to come and see what I can do by the mind of my heavenly father.

"I am"
the master of my cells.

I now focus on my opportunity. I have the power to create my own right to be recognised for my skills and talents.

Let my body of cells show me as capable and trustworthy to whoever I need to work for.

I have the power to create a career that will put me in favour.

My life force is balanced. I know I have this career already before me.

I will be united with and right for everyone's needs.

"I am"
focussed to create an improved me.

This will win me a place within an opportunity I deserve. Let me focus within myself and bring out my doubts and fears.

I shall then deal with them successfully by myself. This shall then place me before others as a trusted colleague ready and able to work and not be hampered by doubts and fears.

No failure will take my dreams from me, or the ability to become who I will be.

I love myself therefore I shall live to show others my greatest ambitions all come true.

"I am"
the master of my cells.

I am now focussed on making my dream come true. Let me take my life-force into my heart feelings where I will hold onto the plan that will give me this wonderful fulfilment.

I have already seen the plan before my eyes. I know that my every need will be met with approval from my peers and relations.

My dreams coming true will not stop theirs coming true for themselves.

We shall then all love the power of the "I am" and enjoy a successful future involving us all, happily bonded together.

"I am"
the master of my cells.

I now have access to my goal. I now ask my body of cells to join me in gaining this goal.

Let each cell grow to play for me. Let each cell react to what I think. I love these cells, for they are given to me from the Forefather's sacred dreams, founded on earth by the power of life.

Let me then unite the spirit of their souls and make them work through me as I focus with the uniqueness of this present time when life will be lived to its fullest.

"I am" one with every seeded cell they passed on to me, thus we are justified to be cloned as the oneness of infinity.

"I am"

the fountain of life that made me look for the reality of who "I am".

I understand I am the consciousness of many light years that passed through good and evil.

I am aware and alert to spiritual demons that cling if I allow them. I also have my forefathers' values but this is my lifetime and I will cleanse all demons successfully.

"I am" part of everything, even from every nation.

I am here to fulfil a masterminded plan, to clean the demons out of my life force and also the life force of my people.

"I am"
the reality of the passing of time.

I possess the fountain of life that re-births the future from the past. Allow me to hold my forefathers' dreams with respect. Allow me to walk with their genes inside me, but cured of the diseases that killed them and would kill me too.

Let me dwell with the angels of light and make my life-force be united with their powers.

"I am" then the future that will make the promises of life come true. Let everyone around me see the light through me and relate with me.

"I am" then no threat to their integrity or beliefs.

***"I am"
the master of my cells.***

My inner child copies my behaviour. I now work with my inner child, allowing it to develop and grow up.

Now I will be an adult with my inner child, and then it will not be childish and needy.

The lost child inside asking for help and direction is me. Let me create light and move from the past into a new future.

I have greater things to learn when I allow myself to grow up and take responsibility for my own failings.

Let all emotions now flow as though I have found the answers to all my questions.

This I have done by myself, therefore everyone around me will know I have grown up and matured.

"I am"
the light body of the soul

This has marked each phase of my trials into the Book of Life. I have the cures inside me when I accept that the problems are mine.

Let me now ask my Forefather's genes not to burden my life with their Karmic paybacks.

Let every cell unite in a new lifetime for me. Therefore, the records of the dead that previously cursed me can now be openly presented to the world, through me, without harming me.

Let me then know that I have this lifetime to do so.

"I am"

the soul consciousness of my higher self.

This allows me to live outside physical pain. I now ask every cell within my body to collect all the energy my soul can give.

This will allow each cell to multiply its life-force. This trade with the soul gives my body time to repair.

Allow me to let go of my fears and know that I am worthy of all the soul can create for me.

Give me then the result of being who "I am" as I achieve my wellbeing.

I have the greatest power then to become whoever I choose.

"I am"

the consciousness of my higher self, united with the soul seeds of my human being.

I am also united with the atoms of the earth. This gives my body the freedom to walk through each challenge with respect for creation.

"I am" flesh and blood that has the skills to unite energy and light. I can gather these fleshly cells together by thought.

I will then use this flesh to create speed, sound and light, using the oils of life to make my dreams come true.

"I am"

the vision of life that has cradled my soul through many times and human bodies.

I have the gifts of the forefathers inside every cell. The soul is a weightless connection between the two, until I invite it to dwell in my dreams.

Allow me to use my cells wisely while I am on this earth, so that through the upper room of my brain that holds my higher self, I can communicate with my light angels.

I can ask for their assistance to produce the materialisation of my dreams. Allow every muscle in my body to work in harmony to present the beauty of my soul in my features.

Then I can gather the star seeds that are rightfully mine.

"I am"
inside my soul's feelings.

Through my soul I will feel my heart beat. This allows every cell within me to be lifted out of emotional discomfort and pain.

Let my movement be free through the use of hydraulic body fluids. Let my energy flow through my glands and adrenals.

I have the time and space available to live out my dreams. I know and believe this can include a life plan.

So let this lifetime form this plan and through me allow it to come true.

"I am"

marred within my human destiny by tragedy and mishap, until I discover I have body, mind and soul.

Let them now bond with the Holy Ghost, being the records of the DNA to remove this deformity from my genetic lineage. Therefore my offspring will also be cleansed.

I now reinforce the three as one and redeem my human spirit from its demons.

I can then resurrect perfection in everything I do. Then shall the earth's karmic laws be rescinded by love.

I can then go free to plan to be whoever I want to be.

"I am"

the son or daughter of the God, creator of every living action.

I have the right to the holy, spiritual trust fund. Let me blend the flesh of my human body with the spiritual echo of this family trust.

Let me keep it sacred and use it to its highest potential, using my all to create perfection.

I love the understanding that my father's seed is of me and through me. Let my dreams focus on the centre of all consciousness.

There I shall find all of everything and use it to achieve a wonderful performance.

I happily accept this task that has been allotted to me at this time.

"I am"

the consciousness of many things.

I know of all things. I live by ordinary values until I focus on the Inner Child and ask it to grow up.

Then I will learn what I already know. When my Inner Child reveals what it knows, I shall grow on this child's behalf.

I will bring my dreams to the surface and use them. Let everything in this world of adventure be mine to walk on or through.

"I am" the form of my new ability as I mature the child in me.

We are now both equal and wise.

"I am"
a righteous human being.

My pain and fear must now go. I now love myself and reject all powers that robbed me of my self esteem.

I now claim my uniqueness as the holder of my genetic lineage. This allows me to walk away from harmful spiritual influences.

Let my heart and my mind now unload the emotional blackness of deep seated genetic memories and form in me the gift of light, love, and reconciliation with the spirits. Therefore I am now successful in my human form.

I am free to work with my beliefs and use my heart to set myself free of past sins and calamities.

I am wholly me.

"I am"

the power of the soul on this earth.

I have access to the higher seeds of all learning. I have a subconscious who can explain the power of time.

The visions of my mind, body and soul are focused within the human spirit. Let love and laughter bring the soul into reality and allow the body, through the mind, to make every cell feel good.

I will focus my senses on becoming the principle of light that will shine out from my clay cells. I will mould them to perfection using my life-force and my inner light.

"I am" then a focused being of light blending past, present and future.

I am the best of everything I intended to be, formed whole in body, mind and soul.

"I am"
the master of my cells.

My physical form is made of clay. I am also both spirit and soul, introduced through the crown of life. I can remodel the clay cells by an order created from my mind through this crown of destiny.

Let me focus on who "I am" and in this body of clay. Blend the soul into a light cell. Let the light body grow from my modelled clay cells and do what the light body formed itself to do.

I fear not, nor would I be harmed by danger or fate. Luck shall not carry me over the brink of time. No, "I am" balanced as if a safety fence surrounded me.

This light body will keep me out of harm's way. "I am" completely encased, away from all harming powers.

I will now be and do what is right for me.

"I am"

a traveller with the spiritual carers until I form the light body around myself.

I will create from the images in my dreams, when I have made this body of light for myself.

"I am" the replica of the Principles of Life. From the very beginning, I was given this space in time.

I now turn my responsibility into action. This will allow me to become acquainted with the celestial beings during my earthly journey.

I am physical but I can build my light body that is fully equipped to protect me against warring spirits and angels.

I can then accept that I shall never grow older or weary in this light body.

It is the resurrection being formed in me.

Self Help Stress Releases

The consciousness of our human power senses a connection with our intuition and personal feelings.

Where the bowerbird of all emotions gathers and where the freedom of our own spirit is condensed by these emotions until it is clarified by the human being.

We ask the feelings of every cell to gather strength and spirit from the human spirit. We are a unique human being that deserves the best from all our emotions.

All the side effects of the negativity of these emotions now must leave the body and I replace them and surround the body with happiness created by;

Love, Joy, Grace, Peace and Wisdom.

I ask my body to relax.

Allow me to relax into the centre of every cell. I now ask for every cell to harmonically correct my health and my emotional feelings until all cells are healthy.

Allow me to feed these cells on my five instincts, having access to all elements, minerals, trace elements and vitamins.

Protect me against any chemical pollutions, additives or toxic influences.

Allow my hormones to be healthy and active. Allow my cells to absorb oxygen and allow me to breathe out the carbon dioxide.

Change any negative emotions into positive ones. Allow my posture to re-establish my personality so that I can attract personal growth in all areas of my life.

I am now the consciousness of my higher self in touch with my human aura.

Therefore the influences of my own selected gifts are reflected in vivid colours and energies.

I am the human cells but I also will create my human spirit to surround me with Love, Joy Grace, Peace and Wisdom.

I ask the body to totally relax. Allow the capabilities of the gland functions to reframe the emotional attraction of the worry and relax and remove it from the body.

Allow the sensitive feelings to let go of the consequences of the worry.

Allow my positive faith to be active and confirm that the mind is free of every part of the worry.

I am then free to have no worry, filling its space with my own confidence and trust.

I am free of all worry.

I ask my body to relax and for my left/right brain to coordinate intuition and intelligence.

Allow the mechanical value of anger to understand the fierceness of its powers, but allow no other emotions to get involved.

Therefore anger becomes its own friend or foe without any obligation to store any other emotions in my mind.

Let me make a joke of anger then let it go.

Do not feel obligated for forgiveness.

Inside the center of our personal attraction to experience our lifetime lessons do not feel obligated to the energy of forgiveness.

Allow the experience to be sealed by the learned parts of the soul that created and influenced the experience and allowed the human to be unscarred in the process.

Inside the centre of my own personal soul, that was blessed by the carriage of conception to pass through the gestation of the human, allow me to bless the womb that carried nurtured and cherished who I was to be.

Allow the feelings that are cross-examined every day to drop all emotions and establish a peace of mind that is a gift of infinite love, stronger than death on the earth.

Ask **my** ***body to relax. Into the center of every cell allow my body to relax.***

Inside the creative thought of every cell, I now formulate my infinite confidence outside egotistical traces.

Allow the truth of my personality understand that I am who I am and to value the capabilities that I own.

Allow me to feel not threatened outside the walls of the cells and therefore the completeness and the uniqueness of every cell is trillions and trillions of me being myself, uplifting me and translating all that I am into a light form for the power and the presence of peace.

Allow every past tense in the presence of the cells to let go of the egotistical grammar of my speech and take into my own intent to the writings I am to be honored to translate for the power of peace.

Allow every organ in this body to work in co-ordination with its cells that are now programmed to accept their duty and to work harmonically with good wealth inside wisdom.

The scenes of my own selfishness that would cause me to feel insecure are now transformed from the audition of a victim to be the choreography of a hero, therefore training me by my own self to play, to dance, and use the mystic form of the Golden Age.

I am free without egotistical energy inside my body, mind and my soul.

My forefathers' seed was chosen by my soul to give me the prestige of my own inheritance to visit the earth as a human with gifts and talents on that family tree.

Allow me to choose the fruit of my inheritance, understanding that this time is ripe to take the fruit and use it wisely.

I am free to inherit the Golden Age.

I am the power of my own values. Therefore I must know that all my depression is as the way I think to value my time and life force.

Deep inside my feelings this depression is a matter formed by the impressions of my personal thinking. To ask it to leave, I must never take another's actions as worry, commitments or judgments.

Allow this day to open for me my right to be me and not caught up with depressed thinking.

I ask the chemicals of my brain to balance the flow of energies throughout this day.

Therefore I am not wasting the power of me, but using the personal instinct with love and healing.

I am now me without entities or cursed worries

I am free.

Before reading this stress release, think about lighting up a cigarette.

Allow the body to totally relax.

Allow the cells to smell the tobacco, to taste it and draw it into the lungs and breathe out the residue.

Allow the pancreas to react and send messages to the pituitary gland to secrete the impact and effects to all of the body.

Allow this body to take full responsibility to carry this feeling from this moment on without a cigarette involved. This allows the physical habit not to be pressured to take and smoke a cigarette.

I am now free without entities or cursed worries. I am free.